DESIGN AND ENGINEERING

BUILDINGS

Alex Woolf

Raintree is an imprint of Capstone Global Library Limited, a company incorporated in England and Wales having its registered office at 7 Pilgrim Street, London, EC4V 6LB – Registered company number: 6695582

To contact Raintree please phone 0845 6044371, fax + 44 (0)1865 312263, or email myorders@raintreepublishers.co.uk. Customers from outside the UK please telephone +44 1865 312262.

Edited by Andrew Farrow, Abby Colich, and
  Vaarunika Dharmapala
Designed by Richard Parker
Original illustrations © Capstone Global Library
  Ltd 2013
Illustrations by HL Studios
Picture research by Elizabeth Alexander
Originated by Capstone Global Library Ltd
Printed and bound in China by CTPS

ISBN 978 1 406 24973 6
16 15 14 13 12
10 9 8 7 6 5 4 3 2 1

British Library Cataloguing in Publication Data
Woolf, Alex.
Buildings. -- (Design and engineering)
690-dc23
A full catalogue record for this book is available from the British Library.

Acknowledgements
We would like to thank the following for permission to reproduce photographs: Alamy pp. 4 (© Stan Rohrer), 10 (© LatitudeStock), 13 (© Construction Photography), 15 (© Chris Howes/Wild Places Photography), 16 (© imagebroker), 19 (© APS [UK]), 20 (© Victor Zastolskiy), 22 (© Aurora Photos), 28 (© Phil Degginger), 29 (© Dan Lee), 30 (© Ashley Cooper pics), 34 (© Michael Doolittle), 38 (© Peter Titmuss), 42 (© Jelle v.d. Wolf), 43 (© Caro), 44 (© Scott Nodine), 47 (© AfriPics.com), 49 (© Iain Masterton), 51 (© Mary Evans Picture Library); © Virtual Building Logistics, LLC p. 40; © Assassi, Photographs Courtesy of BNIM p. 39; © Bill Bradley p. 23; Getty Images pp. 7 (Hulton Archive), 24 (John Burke/Photolibrary), 25 (Frank Perry/AFP), 33 (Joe Robbins), 45 (Associated Newspapers/Daily Mail), 46 (Sean Gallup); Shutterstock pp. 5 (© Nickolay Stanev), 11 (© Pecold), 12 (© Dmitry Kalinovsky), 14 (© clearviewstock), 14 (© Petr Novotny), 18 (© gwycech), 27 (© Parnumas Na Phatthalung), 31 (© Sabri Deniz Kizil), 32 (© Sue Ashe); design feature arrows Shutterstock (© MisterElements).

Cover photograph of the Swiss Re HQ building by Foster + Partners, London, England reproduced with permission of Superstock (© Steve Vidler).

CONTENTS

Some words are shown in bold, **like this**. You can find out what they mean by looking in the glossary.

DESIGNING AND MAKING BUILDINGS

We spend a lot of our lives in buildings, although hardly any of us think too much about how they came to be created.

Before we get into that, let us first try to establish exactly what we mean by a building. A building used to be defined as any human-made structure that has a roof and walls and stands permanently in one place. These days, that definition no longer holds in all cases. Today, it is possible to find portable buildings (see panel on page 5). Also, some modern buildings are dome-shaped, so do not strictly have a roof and walls.

The "Basket Building" in Newark, Ohio, USA, is the headquarters of the Longaberger Company, a manufacturer of (surprise, surprise!) baskets.

The one factor that unites all buildings is that they have to be designed. The art of designing a building is called architecture. The architecture of a building depends on its function and the needs of its users, as well as how much money there is for construction (the budget) and what building materials are available. Architecture is also influenced by changing fashions.

Early buildings

It was around 3500 BC that the first large-scale buildings were constructed, including enormous stone pyramids and temples in Mesopotamia and Egypt. During the Classical Era, which occurred in Europe and the Mediterranean from 800 BC to AD 500, buildings were made according to mathematical rules.

The Taj Mahal in Agra, India, is one of the most universally admired buildings in the world.

The modern era

Over the last 200 years, building designs have been transformed by industrialization, new materials, and mass-production techniques.

Perhaps the greatest innovation of the late 19th and 20th centuries has been the skyscraper. These tall, multi-storey buildings were made possible by the use of steel frameworks from which walls were suspended. Before that, walls were always used to support the weight of upper storeys. As construction technology has improved, skyscrapers have become taller and taller. Today, the tallest building in the world is the Burj Khalifa in Dubai, which stands at 828 metres (2,716 feet).

PORTABLE BUILDINGS

A portable building is one designed to be moveable rather than located permanently in one place. Today, many portable buildings are modular, which means they consist of many modules (sections). These modules are delivered from a factory and then assembled on site. This saves money and produces less construction waste. They can be built in remote locations where it is harder to build conventionally. They are also easily adapted by adding, moving, or removing modules.

Important terms

There are a number of concepts that lie at the heart of building design and construction. They are important to understand before reading this book. Some of these concepts are explained below.

Life cycle

Like all things natural or made, buildings have life cycles. Today, architects design for a building's entire life cycle, from construction to demolition. For example, lighting and heating systems are designed to be energy efficient, and materials are chosen for their recyclability.

Architecture

This is the art and practice of designing and constructing buildings. The architecture of a building describes its physical characteristics (shape, colour), as well as its character (inspiring, homely).

Aesthetics

The ancient Roman architect Vitruvius said a building should satisfy three principles: *firmitas* (durability), *utilitas* (function), and *venustas* (beauty). The study of beauty in buildings, as in art, is called aesthetics. The aesthetics of a building can be found in its colours, lines, shapes and proportions, as well as in its context – that is, how well it fits in with its surroundings and its era.

Function

In 1896, US architect Louis Sullivan wrote "form ever follows function" – in other words, the form of a building should be determined by its function, not the other way around. This raises the question, is part of a building's function to please the eye?

Sustainability

Sustainability is about the responsible management of Earth's resources. Uncontrolled extraction of materials through mining or harvesting is unsustainable – if we take this approach, the materials will eventually run out. Sustainability has become important in every sphere of life and work. In the world of architecture and buildings, it means the responsible sourcing of materials, recycling and reusing as much as we can, and making our buildings energy- and water-efficient.

Planning

In most developed countries, **developers** and architects must obtain permission from local or city planning authorities before they are able to build. These authorities regulate how the land in their locality is used and how anything built there will look.

Computer-Aided Design (CAD)

CAD means architects no longer have to draw building plans by hand – that is left to computers. CAD also allows architects to visualize their buildings in 3-D, which can expose problems and conflicts in the layout that are not apparent in a flat drawing.

Architect Louis Sullivan is known as the "father of the skyscraper".

Building Information Modelling (BIM)

BIM offers a detailed 3-D model of a building which can be used at each stage of its life cycle. Builders use BIM to construct the building virtually before building it physically. **Facility managers** use it for maintenance, and demolition teams use it to simulate various methods of demolition.

WHAT IS TECHNOLOGY?

Technology is the process of using technical knowledge to modify natural materials for meeting human needs and wants.

THE LIFE CYCLE OF A BUILDING

Whether we are talking about cars, boats, or televisions, all human-made objects have a "product life cycle". They must first be imagined by someone. Then the product is planned, designed, tested, and built. After that, it is used until worn out or no longer useful. Finally, it is disposed of. Buildings are no exception to this rule.

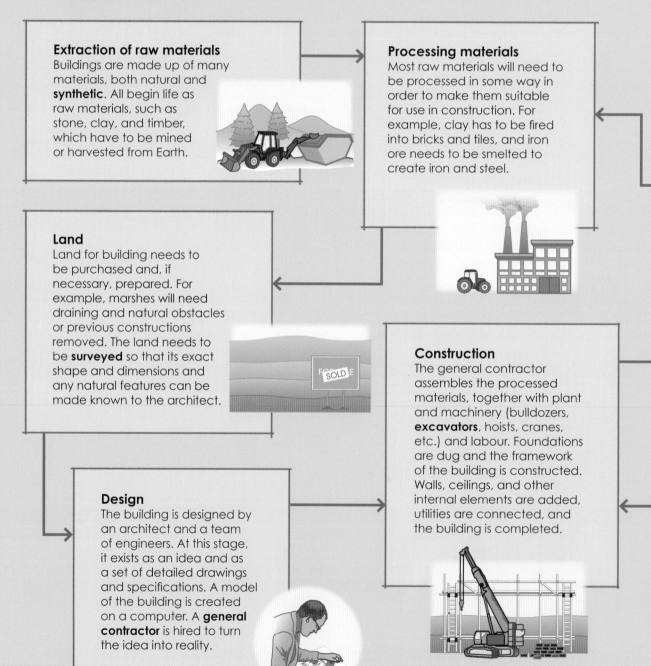

Extraction of raw materials
Buildings are made up of many materials, both natural and **synthetic**. All begin life as raw materials, such as stone, clay, and timber, which have to be mined or harvested from Earth.

Processing materials
Most raw materials will need to be processed in some way in order to make them suitable for use in construction. For example, clay has to be fired into bricks and tiles, and iron ore needs to be smelted to create iron and steel.

Land
Land for building needs to be purchased and, if necessary, prepared. For example, marshes will need draining and natural obstacles or previous constructions removed. The land needs to be **surveyed** so that its exact shape and dimensions and any natural features can be made known to the architect.

Construction
The general contractor assembles the processed materials, together with plant and machinery (bulldozers, **excavators**, hoists, cranes, etc.) and labour. Foundations are dug and the framework of the building is constructed. Walls, ceilings, and other internal elements are added, utilities are connected, and the building is completed.

Design
The building is designed by an architect and a team of engineers. At this stage, it exists as an idea and as a set of detailed drawings and specifications. A model of the building is created on a computer. A **general contractor** is hired to turn the idea into reality.

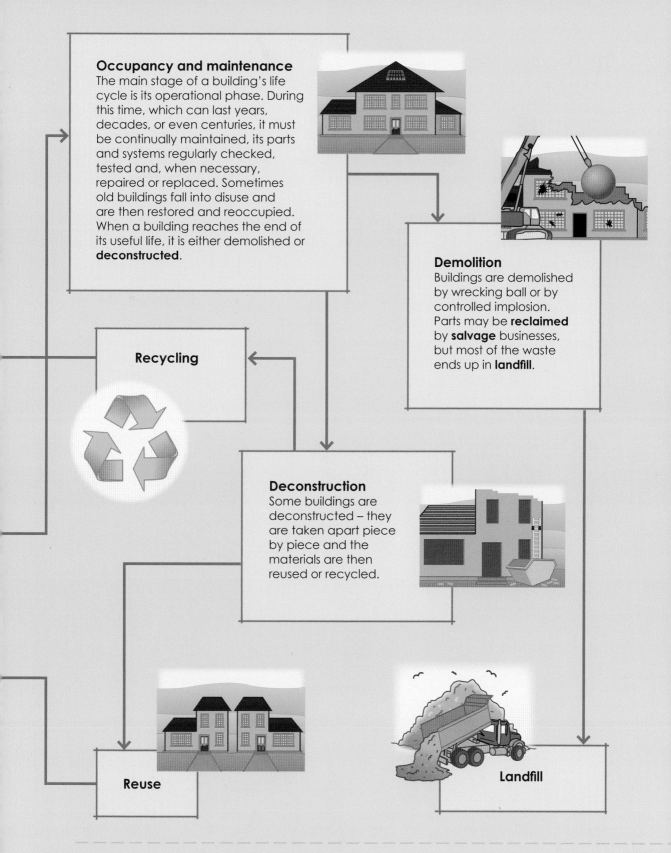

Occupancy and maintenance
The main stage of a building's life cycle is its operational phase. During this time, which can last years, decades, or even centuries, it must be continually maintained, its parts and systems regularly checked, tested and, when necessary, repaired or replaced. Sometimes old buildings fall into disuse and are then restored and reoccupied. When a building reaches the end of its useful life, it is either demolished or **deconstructed**.

Demolition
Buildings are demolished by wrecking ball or by controlled implosion. Parts may be **reclaimed** by **salvage** businesses, but most of the waste ends up in **landfill**.

Recycling

Deconstruction
Some buildings are deconstructed – they are taken apart piece by piece and the materials are then reused or recycled.

Reuse

Landfill

Real-estate development

Before there can be a building, there has to be a piece of vacant land on which to build. A developer buys the land and builds on it with a view to making a profit by selling or renting out the building. Developers must think about where to buy land and what kind of buildings to construct there. They work with many other people during the process of planning and construction, including local planning authorities, **surveyors**, architects, and contractors.

Planning and permissions

The developer must approach the **Local Planning Authority (LPA)** for permission to build on the site. In making its decision, the LPA is usually guided by certain principles, including the following:

- Will the proposed building benefit the local community?
- Will local landscapes or sites of historic, **ecological**, or scientific importance be adversely affected?
- Will it be in keeping with local architectural traditions?
- Will it damage the environment or use up scarce resources?
- Will it be energy efficient?

LPAs generally consult the public before making a decision, particularly people living next door or close to the site. The LPA may ask a developer to make changes to the proposed building before granting permission. Sometimes the developer is asked to contribute towards local **infrastructure** costs – for example, to build a new road linking the building to local amenities.

In some cases, the land on which a building is sited does not even exist at the start of the project. Hong Kong airport, shown here under construction, was built on a specially created artificial island.

The Tower of Hercules stands at 55 metres (180 feet) tall. Since 2009, it has been a UNESCO World Heritage Site.

CONTRAST THE PAST

The life cycle of a building can be long or short, depending on the type of building, the quality of its construction, and whether it remains useful to the community it serves. One of the oldest buildings still in use is the Tower of Hercules. This ancient Roman lighthouse in Galicia, Spain, has been continually in use since it was built in the second century AD. This contrasts with the short lives of many modern buildings. For example, the average lifespan of residential buildings in Beijing, China, is currently 25 to 30 years.

Survey

After permission has been granted to build on a site, the site is surveyed. This is the process of accurately studying, measuring, and mapping the site, including its **topography** (the natural contours of the land), the type of soil (some soils are more suitable for construction than others), and its boundaries. Any natural features, such as waterways, are recorded.

Surveyors use sophisticated equipment to measure distances and to determine height differences and angles between different parts of the site. The equipment includes the total station, an electronic theodolite (angle measurer) combined with an electronic distance meter to measure slope distances. Robotic total stations allow operators to control them from a distance. The operator can stand at another part of the site with a reflector. The total station bounces light pulses off the reflector to determine distance.

Robotic total stations can measure both distances and the angles of slopes. This helps the surveyor to chart the topography of a building site.

Design

Once the site is surveyed, the designing of the building can commence. This is carried out by an architect. The developer briefs the architect on the details of the planned project. The architect prepares a design concept, including construction drawings and specifications. Architects usually work with specialists, such as structural and mechanical engineers, in order to provide the developer with as detailed a plan as possible. Architects must make sure their designs comply with local building codes and regulations.

Construction

Once the design has been approved, the developer (or the architect working on the developer's behalf) hires a general contractor to carry out the construction. The general contractor is responsible for the day-to-day running of the construction site, and provides the necessary materials, labour, engineering equipment, tools, and services. The general contractor hires **subcontractors** to carry out each aspect of the job, including carpentry and security. The developer, architect, and general contractor work closely together to meet deadlines and budget.

ECO IMPACT

The construction industry is thought to be responsible for 40 per cent of all environmental damage in the European Union and the United States. Each phase in a building's life cycle has a different kind of environmental impact.

One study, looking at office buildings, found that the most damaging impact of the construction phase was summer smog and a build-up of **heavy metals** in the environment. Summer smog is caused, in part, by the release of nitrogen oxide into the atmosphere. Heavy metals include mercury, cadmium, lead, and chromium. Both nitrogen oxide and heavy metals are emitted during the manufacturing process of building materials.

The most damaging impact of the operational phase of an office building's life was **acidification** (of soil and water) and eutrophication (addition of nitrates and phosphates through sewage into the water system). The study found that the biggest causes of environmental damage during an office building's life were its electricity use, HVAC (heating, ventilation, and air conditioning), and its use of water and wastewater. For more on the environmental impact of building materials, see page 54.

This model of the London skyline shows towering office buildings. These contribute significantly to environmental pollution.

Operation and maintenance

After the building has been constructed, it passes into the main stage of its life cycle: the operational phase. During this phase the building must be continually maintained. This job is done by a facility manager, who carries out regular tests and inspections on the building's working parts to ensure they are operating correctly.

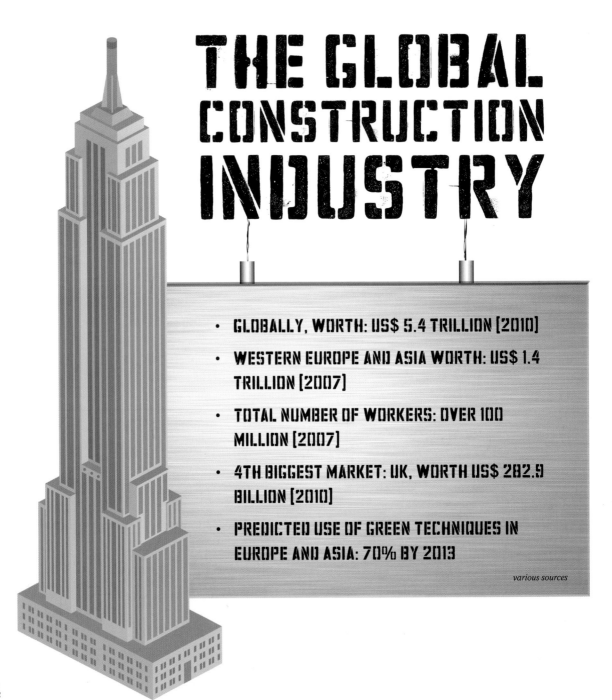

THE GLOBAL CONSTRUCTION INDUSTRY

- GLOBALLY, WORTH: US$ 5.4 TRILLION [2010]

- WESTERN EUROPE AND ASIA WORTH: US$ 1.4 TRILLION [2007]

- TOTAL NUMBER OF WORKERS: OVER 100 MILLION [2007]

- 4TH BIGGEST MARKET: UK, WORTH US$ 282.9 BILLION [2010]

- PREDICTED USE OF GREEN TECHNIQUES IN EUROPE AND ASIA: 70% BY 2013

various sources

Demolition

At some point, the owners of a building will decide it has served its useful purpose and should be demolished. There are many possible reasons for this – the building may have deteriorated physically to the point that it is no longer cost-effective to keep maintaining it; the neighbourhood may have changed in character, rendering the building obsolete; or the land on which it sits may have become sufficiently valuable to attract a developer who wishes to use the site for another purpose.

Buildings are usually demolished by means of **hydraulic** excavators, bulldozers, and cranes fitted with wrecking balls. Large buildings may be demolished by a controlled implosion, using explosives (see pages 46–47). A greener approach to demolition, known as deconstruction, involves dismantling the building and sorting its components for reuse or recycling.

Salvage, reclamation, and recycling of materials

The demolition of a building does not necessarily mean the end for its component materials. Salvage businesses reclaim materials such as stone, as well as ornamental pieces such as antique bathrooms. These are then sold on and incorporated into new buildings.

Bath and plumbing fixtures can be salvaged from buildings marked for demolition.

WHAT HAVE WE LEARNED?
- Developers obtain permission to build.
- Surveyors establish the topography of the land.
- Architects produce detailed designs of the proposed building.
- A general contractor oversees construction of the building.
- A facility manager maintains the building during its operational phase.
- At the end of a building's life, it is demolished or deconstructed.

DESIGNING A BUILDING

Buildings are complex structures, and planning and designing them requires input from a range of professionals. Initially, the client, usually a developer, approaches an architect. The client briefs the architect on exactly what sort of building is required. The architect may be asked to prepare a **feasibility study**, looking at the strengths and weaknesses of the proposed building.

The design team

To help prepare the design, the architect assembles a team of experts:

- *Structural engineers*, who specialize in the analysis and design of, for example, walls and floors that support or resist loads. Their job is to ensure the building will not collapse as a result of occupation, weather, or natural disasters.
- *Mechanical engineers*, who specialize in the mechanical, electrical, heating, air conditioning, and plumbing systems.
- *Draughtspeople*, whose job is to prepare technical drawings using CAD, in order to visually represent how the finished building will look.
- *A quantity surveyor*, whose role is to measure and control the costs of the construction project, to ensure the client obtains good value.
- *An environmental consultant*, who ensures the design complies with local environmental regulations. For example, they advise on what kinds of building materials can be used and how to deal with building waste.

This architect is using CAD to design display booths for a large exhibition hall.

Creating the design

It is the job of the architect, with help from the design team, to create a design that meets the client's requirements and budget, fits the purpose intended for the building, and provides a secure, safe, and healthy environment for its occupants. When creating a design, the architect must take account of the surveyor's report on the size, topography, and condition of the site, and must also comply with local planning laws and regulations.

Beyond these specific considerations, architects will usually bear in mind several broader factors. These vary in importance, depending on the type of project and the architect's own views. They include:

- *Social impact*: how will the building be received in the local community? Will it fit in with its immediate surroundings?
- *Environmental impact*: what materials can be used to minimize damage to the environment? How can the building be made energy efficient?
- *Aesthetics*: is the design attractive? Will the building fit with the architectural fashions of the era?

It is not always possible to fulfil all these requirements within the scope of the client's budget and brief. In such cases, the architect must choose which factors are most important and prioritize those.

BUILDING TALK

"Every great architect is – necessarily – a great poet. He must be a great original interpreter of his time, his day, his age."
Frank Lloyd Wright (1867–1959)

"Architecture is basically a container of something. I hope they will enjoy not so much the teacup, but the tea."
Yoshio Taniguchi (born 1937)

Architectural drawings

Architects produce technical drawings of the proposed building at all stages of the design process. These are used to develop initial ideas, to communicate these ideas to colleagues, to convince the client of the merits of a design, to help a general contractor to construct it, and, finally, to make a record of the completed building. Architectural drawings take several different forms:

- *Floor plan*: diagram of the view from above a floor of the building, showing the layout of rooms, much like a map.
- *Site plan*: another bird's-eye-view diagram, showing the entire site, and sometimes the surrounding landscape. It shows the site boundaries, as well as natural and built features (such as trees, roads, and footpaths) and connections to drainage and sewer pipes, water supply, and electrical and communications cables.
- *Elevation*: shows a view of the building seen from one side. It is used to show the external appearance of a building.
- *Cross section*: shows a vertical slice through the building. Cross sections help to show the relationship between different levels of a building.
- *Roof plan*: shows the shape of the roof. It specifies aspects such as the roofing materials, the structure of the roof frame, ventilation outlets, and drainage. Roof plans are usually drawn on the same sheet as the elevations.

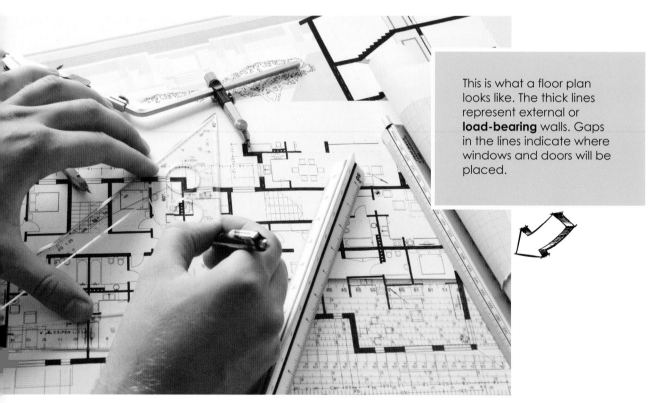

This is what a floor plan looks like. The thick lines represent external or **load-bearing** walls. Gaps in the lines indicate where windows and doors will be placed.

Case study: hospitals

An architect commissioned to design a hospital must think about the particular needs of such an institution. For example, distances from ward to scanning room or operating theatre should be minimized to increase efficiency and reduce travel times for patients and staff.

However well planned, most hospital buildings eventually outgrow the visions of their founders. New sections are added in a haphazard fashion according to need and the availability of finance. This has prompted Dutch architectural historian Cor Wagenaar to describe many hospitals as "built catastrophes, anonymous institutional complexes run by vast bureaucracies, and totally unfit for the purpose they have been designed for ... They are hardly ever functional, and instead of making patients feel at home, they produce stress and anxiety."

Architects of many modern hospitals have placed greater emphasis on patient needs, providing them with access to fresh air, pleasant surroundings, and natural light. Sometimes the needs of patients need to be balanced against those of staff. For example, many medical staff prefer to accommodate patients in wards because it allows them to do their jobs more efficiently. However, some patients regard wards as stressful and lacking in privacy.

To learn more about the special challenges involved in hospital construction, watch this video: www.youtube.com/watch?v=ul2MGgh3JCA.

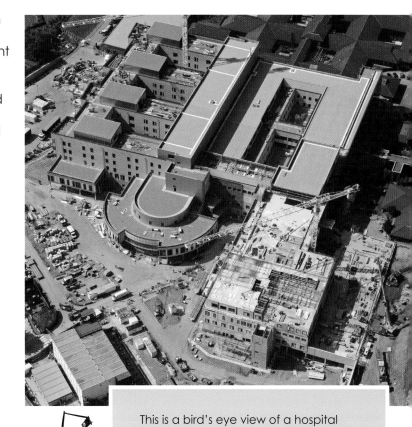

This is a bird's eye view of a hospital under construction. Modern hospitals are large, complex structures with many interlinked departments.

Computer-Aided Design (CAD)

Today, most architectural drawings are created electronically, using CAD. There are many advantages to this approach:

- Drawings can be produced quickly.
- Architectural features can be copied, reducing repetition.
- Errors are easily deleted.
- Variations can be tried out before the design is finalized.
- Revisions can quickly be sent to the client on site, using mobile technology.

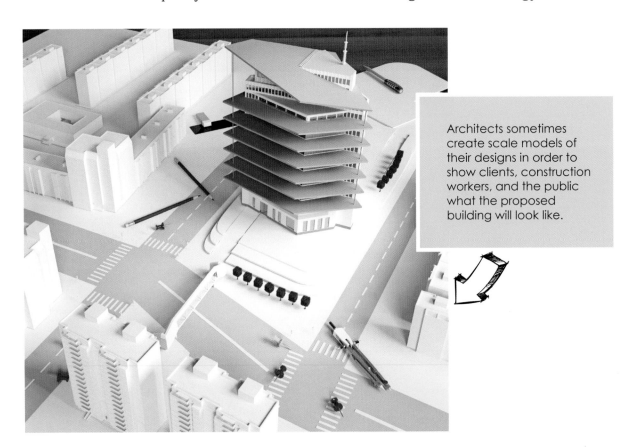

Architects sometimes create scale models of their designs in order to show clients, construction workers, and the public what the proposed building will look like.

In fact, CAD has made the process of design so convenient that architects can sometimes lose sight of what is practical when it comes to construction. CAD encourages architects to add greater complexity to their designs, and it can raise expectations of accuracy.

As well as technical drawings, CAD is used to create photorealistic views of the finished building for showing to the client or the public. CAD software can generate 3-D models of the building that can be viewed from any direction. It can even produce animated films, featuring people and cars, to show how the building might look when in use.

Sustainable architecture

It cannot be denied that buildings have a major impact on the environment. For example, in the United States in 2005, buildings contributed 38.9 per cent of the nation's total **carbon dioxide** emissions. Under pressure from international organizations, governments, and lobbyists, most modern architects seek to minimize the environmental cost of their buildings. This approach, known as **sustainable** architecture, looks at ways of increasing energy efficiency, using **renewable** forms of energy and recycled materials.

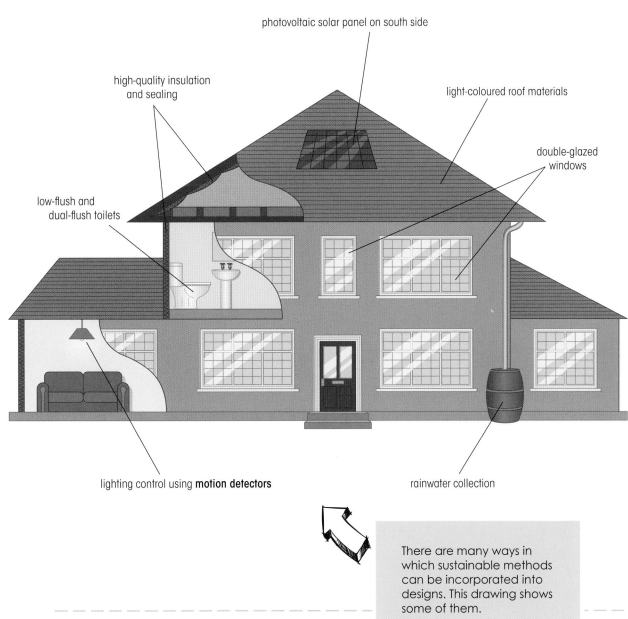

photovoltaic solar panel on south side

high-quality insulation and sealing

light-coloured roof materials

double-glazed windows

low-flush and dual-flush toilets

lighting control using **motion detectors**

rainwater collection

There are many ways in which sustainable methods can be incorporated into designs. This drawing shows some of them.

21

Local factors

In some places, architects face the challenge of designing buildings that can withstand natural disasters, such as earthquakes, floods, and hurricanes.

Earthquake engineering

Most buildings in quake-prone regions incorporate some form of earthquake-resistant engineering. For example, "**seismic** vibration control" devices may be installed to reduce the impact of shock waves. These are usually dampers – concrete or steel blocks that move in opposition to the shock waves by means of springs, fluids, or pendulums. Another technique is "base isolation", which involves inserting pads into or beneath all major load-bearing supports in the base of the building. This isolates the main part of the building from its foundations, reducing the impact of the quake.

Earthquake engineers often test structures, building materials, and components on "shaking tables" like this one.

Earthquake engineers also look at ways of reinforcing the structure itself. Steel is considered relatively earthquake resistant, and concrete or **masonry** can be made less brittle by reinforcing it with steel. Some structures are "prestressed" (they contain permanent stresses) in order to improve their performance during quakes.

Building in flood-prone regions

Floodwater is damaging, expensive, and can carry disease. In some flood-prone areas, buildings make use of waterproof materials for the frame, panels, floors, and walls. Doors and other access points are guarded, and waterproof sealants used to dry-proof the building. Pipes allow floodwater to drain away.

In poverty-stricken Bangladesh, where flooding is frequent, people find simple, cost-effective methods to protect their homes. Some construct concrete plinths to prevent homes being washed away; they use replaceable jute panels for walls, and bracings and fastenings to bind the walls to the house skeleton – known locally as the clam system; they also plant water-thirsty vegetation around the house to absorb floodwater.

Hurricane-proof architecture

Architects in hurricane-prone areas bear in mind the destructive effects of high winds. To reduce the possibility of the roof being torn off, it needs to be anchored, via the walls, to the building's foundation. Architects might also consider the shape of the building: dome roofs or buildings that are low to the ground are better able to withstand high winds than tall or square buildings.

Roof **trusses** are secured to the tops of walls using special connectors called hurricane ties.

WHAT HAVE WE LEARNED?
- Architects work with a team of specialists.
- They consider the client's requirements, the health and safety of the users, and the physical layout of the site.
- Architects produce technical drawings using CAD.
- Sustainable architecture aims at reducing environmental cost.
- Architects must design their buildings to withstand local conditions.

MATERIALS

Buildings are constructed using a wide range of materials, including naturally occurring ones such as clay and stone, and synthetic substances such as concrete, foam, and fabric. The mining, harvesting, manufacture, and processing of building materials is a global industry, predicted to be worth US$706.7 billion by 2015. Governments and environmental groups are increasingly concerned about the sustainability of certain materials and the damage their extraction causes to the environment.

Clay

Clay is used to create many traditional building materials, including **adobe**, rammed earth, and wattle and daub, as well as plaster, clay floors, and clay paints. Clay is a useful substance because, like stone (but unlike wood), it retains heat, releasing it over a period of time. This keeps homes cool in the summer and warm in winter. It is also exceptionally durable: clay bricks and roof tiles can be seen today in buildings constructed by the ancient Romans.

This timber is being cut to be used in the construction industry. Sawdust and other sawmill waste is made into particleboard, used to make doors, stair treads, and countertops.

Wood

Buildings have been made of wood for thousands of years. Wood constructions require relatively little labour and can be very attractive. On the down side, they do not retain heat well, present a fire risk, and lack durability. Despite this, wood remains important in modern construction, both as a structural and an aesthetic material. Many new homes have a timber frame, wooden doors, frames, shutters, and sills.

Metal

Metal is used as the framework or external surface covering of many large buildings. The most commonly used metal in construction is steel, an **alloy** of iron that possesses the ideal properties of a construction material: strength, flexibility, and durability. The disadvantage of steel is its tendency to corrode over time. Aluminium alloys, titanium, and tin resist corrosion better than steel, but are more expensive. Other metals, such as chrome and silver, are used decoratively.

This building in the Parc du Futuroscope, near Poitiers, France, is an impressive example of the reflective qualities of glass.

CONTRAST THE PAST

Glass is usually made from a mixture of sand and silicates (a type of mineral) heated in a kiln. It is brittle, but its key property is its transparency. The invention of glass allowed people to let light into their homes while keeping the elements out. Originally, glass windows were few in number and small because glass was expensive to produce. Today, glass is widely used. Many public buildings feature glass "curtain walls" or glass roofs known as space frames, in which large sections of glass are placed within a frame. These features lend the buildings a sense of light and space. The Louvre Pyramid, designed by architect I. M. Pei and completed in 1989, is made entirely of glass segments within a metal frame.

Cement

Cement is a binder – a substance that acts like a kind of glue, binding other materials together. The most common kind of cement is Portland Cement, which is used to make mortar, concrete, **stucco**, and grout. In all cases, **aggregates** are bonded by the cement to form a strong building material. Cement sets when mixed with water. The water reacts with the cement, causing its constituents to form interlocking crystals, which gives cement its strength.

ECO IMPACT

There are environmental impacts at all stages in the process of producing Portland Cement. Quarries scar the landscape, and the blasting of the raw materials from the earth causes dust and gas emissions. The processing and heating of the materials releases carbon dioxide into the atmosphere. According to 2007 figures, the cement industry was responsible for over 5 per cent of global human-made carbon dioxide emissions. The heating of some forms of limestone and clay can release toxic heavy metals, such as thallium, mercury, and cadmium, into the atmosphere.

Today, measures are often taken to reduce the environmental damage caused by cement manufacture. These include:

- use of equipment to trap and separate waste gases during quarrying
- restoring old quarries to nature or farmland
- moving cement plants closer to quarries to reduce transport emissions
- development of a new type of "eco-cement", which can absorb carbon dioxide from the air during the hardening process
- use of waste materials and by-products to fuel rotary kilns, instead of coal.

Case study: Portland Cement manufacture

Quarry
Most of the raw materials come from surface mines, although some, such as sand, are dredged from lakes and rivers.

⬇

Crushing/screening plant
Raw materials are crushed and screened to particles of around 19 mm (¾ in) diameter and then stored in a stockpile.

⬇

Ball mill
The particles are ground to powder (in some cases they are wet ground by adding water to form a **slurry**) and then blended according to the manufacturer's "secret recipe".

⬇

Rotary kiln
In the rotary kiln, the blend of raw materials fuse at around 1,482°C (2,700°F) to form small rocks called clinker.

⬇

Ball mill
The clinker is ground to powder and shipped to customers as Portland Cement.

Cement plants are major emitters of pollution, including carbon dioxide (CO_2) – which contributes to global warming – and toxic heavy metals.

Concrete

Concrete is a composite material (containing two or more constituents) made up of aggregate (fragments of broken or crushed stone, gravel, or sand) and a binder – usually cement. Concrete is as strong as stone, long lasting, and easily formable into different shapes. These properties have made it the key building material of modern times. In fact, twice as much concrete is used in construction around the world than the total of all other building materials combined. However, concrete has a low tensile strength (it breaks easily under stress), and so when used as part of a large structure, steel rods, as well as organic and inorganic fibres, are usually added to give it extra strength. This material is called reinforced concrete.

Liquid concrete is poured over rebar (steel rods) to make reinforced concrete. This material is ideal for use in walls, beams, columns, and much more.

Annual global production of building materials

building material	amount produced (approximate)
cement (2010 figure)	3,300,000,000 metric tonnes
concrete (average annual figure)	3,822,774,000 cubic metres
timber (2006 figure)	logs: 1,313,200,000 cubic metres
	sawn wood: 362,200,000 cubic metres
	veneer: 10,200,000 cubic metres
	plywood: 70,000,000 cubic metres
steel (2011 figure)	1,526.9 megatonnes
sheet glass (average annual figure)	6,100,000,000 square metres

Plastic

Plastic is one of the most versatile materials. In its semi-liquid state, it is malleable and can be moulded or cast into objects of any shape. It is light, hard-wearing, and of uniform consistency. As a result, plastic is used extensively in building construction. In the early 20th century, its use was limited to floor coverings and moulded interior features such as door handles. Since the development of acrylic, polythene, PVC, and polystyrene in the 1930s, plastic has found uses as wall panels, paints, cladding, and insulation.

Today, plastics are used as a principal building material. An example of this can be found at the Eden Project in Cornwall. This visitor attraction consists of a series of biomes set in transparent domes housing plants from all around the world. The domes are made up of hexagonal inflated plastic sections held within a steel grid.

Linen is a sustainable material that is increasingly being used in the building industry. Here, flax fibres are being spread in preparation for being made into linen.

Foam

Foam is made by trapping gas in a liquid form of plastic or rubber and then solidifying it. Foam is light and easily formed into different shapes, and is useful as an insulator in buildings. Foam panels are sandwiched between structural components such as wood, plaster, or concrete to help insulate buildings from cold, heat, noise, or fire.

WHAT HAVE WE LEARNED?
- Buildings are made using a wide range of materials.
- Clay keeps interior building temperatures at a constant level.
- Wood remains an important building material.
- Steel is used both as a framework and as a strengthener of concrete.
- Today, glass and plastic are used as structural building materials.
- Modern methods can be used to reduce the environmental cost of cement manufacturing.

CONSTRUCTING A BUILDING

Each type of building requires its own particular method of construction. However, there are some essential principles, common to almost all forms of building construction. In this chapter, we will look at what goes on at a building site and who is employed there.

Site preparation and foundation

The first stage of any construction is to prepare the site. Bulldozers are brought in to clear the site of trees, rocks, and any other obstacles and then to dig a trench for the foundation – the lowest and supporting layer of the building. Trenches are dug to carry cables and pipes to and from the property.

This team is starting work on a beach resort complex in Dubai, UAE. Site preparation on a shoreline will include the removal of large amounts of sand in order to lay the foundation.

The foundation can take the form of a concrete slab, a basement, or a **crawlspace**. Structural engineers must ensure the foundation and the soil beneath it are able to bear the weight of the building. Generally speaking, the weaker the soil or the heavier the building, the deeper the foundation will need to be. Common challenges include the tendency for one part of the foundation to settle more than another, and changes in moisture levels causing clay-based soil to swell or shrink.

ECO IMPACT

The construction industry is adopting many sustainable techniques in the creation of new buildings. These include:

- the use of reused, recycled, or responsibly sourced materials
- the use of materials that are easily recyclable, such as metals and timber
- building to last: the longer a building stands, the better for the environment
- reducing the amount of waste that goes to landfill. According to research carried out by WRAP (Waste & Resources Action Programme), off-site construction, such as creating bathrooms in factories and transporting them to the site, can reduce the amount of on-site waste by up to 90 per cent.

THE ENVIRONMENTAL COST OF BUILDINGS

The Organization for Economic Co-operation and Development (OECD) is a group of countries including economically developed and emerging economies. In OECD countries, the built environment is responsible for:

25-40% OF TOTAL ENERGY USE

30% OF RAW MATERIAL USE

30-40% OF GLOBAL GREENHOUSE GAS EMISSIONS

30-40% OF SOLID WASTE GENERATION

Framing

Once the foundation has been laid, the framework of the building is constructed. This is the building's skeleton, to which interior and exterior walls, floors, ceilings, and the roof are attached (see diagram on page 37). The framework is usually made of wood or steel tubes. It includes vertical wall supports known as studs, horizontal supports for floors and ceilings called joists, and sloping supports for the roof called **rafters**. Diagonal wall and roof supports are called wind braces. Interior walls that support ceiling or roof loads are called load-bearing walls, while others are called partitions.

In timber-framed structures, wall studs are often supported by plywood sheathing to give the wall rigidity. Spaces for doors and windows are created at this stage. Horizontal beams placed over windows and doors, called lintels, support the weight of the structure above.

Once the skeleton of a building has been completed, its shape and size become clear.

Walls and internal features

The next step is to install the windows and external doors, and then to build the exterior walls. At this stage, the larger structural elements inside are created, including pillars and stairs. Plumbing and air conditioning pipes and electrical cabling are installed, and the roof is built. The walls can now be insulated, and **drywall** is nailed or screwed to the wall studs and ceiling joists. Built-in cabinets and counters are constructed, and floorboards, interior doors, stair railings, and other parts are installed.

Case study: building a sports stadium

The world's oldest recorded stadium is in Olympia, Greece, where the ancient Olympics were held from 776 BC. We know little about its construction, but builders of modern sports stadiums face a particular set of challenges.

Stadium builders must consider how best to maximize comfort and visibility for viewers. How should the stadium be positioned to avoid the prevailing winds or glare from the setting Sun? How should columns be placed so they do not obstruct views? What angle of slope should the terrace be given so people at the back can see the action?

Another consideration is where to place the stand exits. Exits at the front can cause trouble if people leave the game early, as it can be off-putting for the rest of the crowd and the players on the pitch. Exits at the back of the stand are more costly as they will require stairs to be built. They may also have an impact on safety in the case of an emergency evacuation, and are not good for disabled access.

The style of roof or canopy needs to be chosen with care. Roofs that slope to the back will give spectators a better view of high balls and are good for drainage, but will let in more rain and wind and produce more shade on the pitch. Some modern stadiums, such as the Millennium Stadium in Cardiff, Wales, have a retractable sliding roof that can cover the entire stadium in the event of rain.

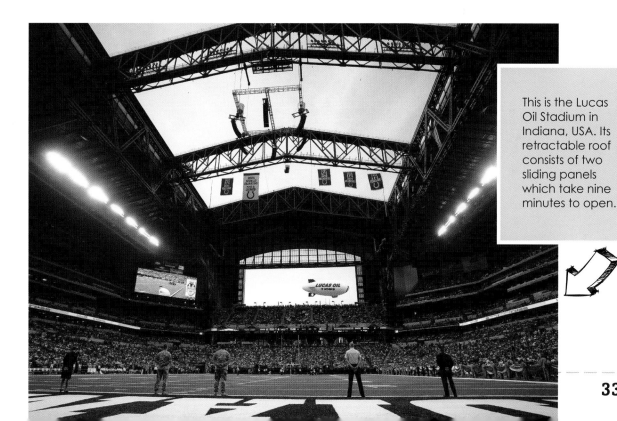

This is the Lucas Oil Stadium in Indiana, USA. Its retractable roof consists of two sliding panels which take nine minutes to open.

Finishing touches

The final stage of construction involves the decorative and functional elements that will turn the building into a place fit for human habitation. This includes painting, tiling the walls or wallpapering, carpeting or applying finish to the floors, and installing essential appliances.

This stage will also involve a final visit from the electrician to install sockets, light fixtures, and doorbells, and from the plumber to install sinks, baths, and toilets.

Plasterers use special tools called screeds, floats, and trowels to achieve a smooth finish on walls and ceilings.

Building site personnel

The general contractor or project manager must hire subcontractors with particular skills to carry out the many different tasks that are needed to make a building. Here are just a few examples of the people who work on a typical building site:

- *Bricklayers*: lay bricks or blocks to make walls. As part of their training, they learn how to cut and lay bricks, and to prepare and apply mortar.
- *Carpenters*: work with timber. In the building trade, they are needed as framers (to build the framework), trim carpenters (to create mouldings and trim such as door or window casings and skirting boards) and formwork carpenters (to create the moulds into which concrete is poured during the construction process).

- *Concrete finishers*: also known as cement masons, responsible for placing, finishing, protecting, and repairing concrete on the construction site. Concrete finishers take newly mixed, still-wet concrete and spread it across a prepared surface. They smooth and level it with a masonry trowel and give it an edge so it is less likely to chip.
- *Ironworkers*: handle most jobs involving metal components on the building site. Using a range of power and manual tools, ironworkers assemble or dismantle steel frames, position reinforcing steel bars in concrete, and erect metal stairs.
- *Plasterers*: work with plaster, creating smooth layers or decorative mouldings on interior ceilings or walls, or rendering exterior walls.
- *Pipefitters*: also known as steamfitters, they work with piping systems. Pipes are essential in all buildings for conveying steam, liquid, water, sewage, fuel, and chemicals.
- *Roofers*: specialize in the construction of roofs. They need carpentry skills to fit the wooden rafters, beams, and trusses that form the roof's skeleton, before installing the cladding (tiles, shingles, metal sheets, or thatch) that protects the building from the elements.

BUILDING TALK

General contractors are sometimes called project managers. Here, one of them talks about his job:

"To be a project manager takes strong communication and technical skills, and a passion for multitasking … It's important to bring people together and help them work towards a common goal … Technology plays a big part in the construction industry [and] has changed how we plan and execute construction projects. The use of computers and modelling has meant time and money saving on all projects … As part of my day I come on to the job site and help with questions and talk to the crews … There is a great sense of accomplishment to see the product of your hard work being put in place."

Jim Yehle, J. H. Findorff & Son
See www.youtube.com/watch?v=5vStHoQJSvc

Construction site safety

Construction is the most hazardous land-based industry in Europe, with 13 workers per 100,000 dying each year, compared to an all-sector average of 5 per 100,000. Common accidents include falls, crashes, excavation accidents, electrocution, and being struck by falling objects. Workers also risk hearing impairment from high noise levels, or may suffer lung problems and even death if exposed to toxic substances such as **asbestos**.

Efforts have been made to improve safety in recent years, including better training for workers and installation of guardrails, safety nets, and warning devices. Vehicles are equipped with emergency brakes and audible warning systems. Regular site inspections are made to assess the risks. As a result, accident rates have declined overall, although some countries' safety records are better than others (see the table below).

Rate of deaths from injuries in construction in 2005*

country	deaths per 100,000 workers	number of deaths	total workforce
Hong Kong	42.2	25	59,266
Italy	11.7	239	2,046,000
United States	11.1	1,243	11,178,000
Spain	9.9	248	2,509,000
Finland	7.0	12	171,000
Germany	6.0	138	2,400,000
Australia	5.9	36	887,000
Switzerland	4.8	13	269,000
Sweden	4.4	11	253,000
United Kingdom	3.5	72	2,069,000

* Most recent statistics available.

Construction completion

The following procedures are carried out before a building can be occupied:

- The local planning authority inspects the building and, if satisfied, issues a safety certificate.
- The construction office is closed and the workers are dismissed.
- The contractor supplies a set of "as-built" drawings, indicating all changes made to the original design; operating manuals for electrical, plumbing, heating, and communications equipment; warranties; and a final report.
- The contractor may be asked to provide training for the building's staff.

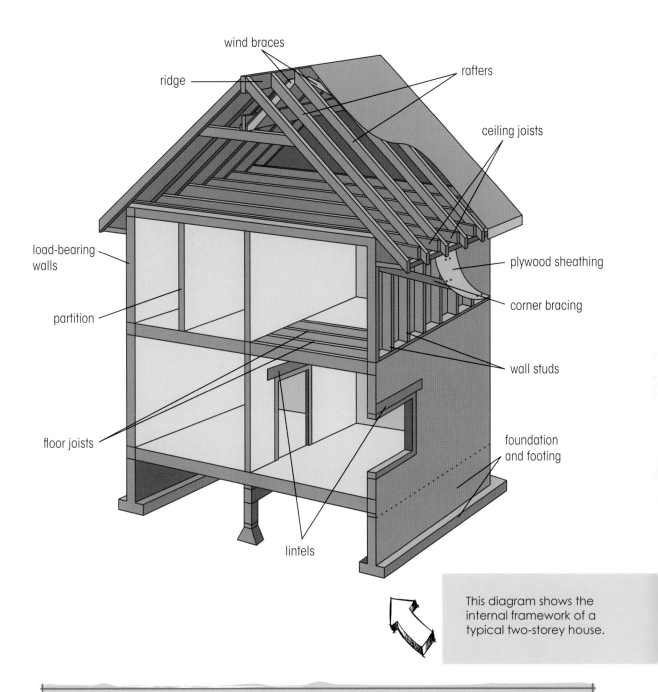

wind braces

ridge

rafters

ceiling joists

load-bearing walls

plywood sheathing

partition

corner bracing

wall studs

floor joists

foundation and footing

lintels

This diagram shows the internal framework of a typical two-storey house.

WHAT HAVE WE LEARNED?
- Construction proceeds in a sequence of stages.
- Building sites employ a range of specialist workers.
- Construction sites are dangerous places, although efforts to improve safety have been effective in some countries.

OPERATING AND MAINTAINING A BUILDING

During the operational phase of a building's life cycle, it must be regularly cleaned and maintained. Its mechanical parts must be serviced and, when necessary, repaired, and its occupants must be kept comfortable and safe from hazards such as floods, fire, and burglary. Occasionally, if there is a structural fault or a problem with the foundations, major repairs must be carried out.

In the case of small buildings such as private houses, the occupants themselves can usually take care of these matters, calling in tradespeople as required. However, with larger buildings such as offices, hospitals, or schools, a facility manager is usually employed to look after the building. In this chapter, we will examine the role of the facility manager.

Maintenance

Part of the facility manager's role is "preventive maintenance" – in other words, arranging regular inspections of plumbing, security, and other systems in order to identify potential problems and make adjustments or replace parts before major breakdowns occur.

These electricians are carrying out repairs in an industrial building.

Case study: facility management at a tax office

A large number of US tax returns are processed at the Internal Revenue Service (IRS) office in Kansas City, USA. This giant building occupies nearly 103,000 square metres (1.1 million square feet) and, during peak times, employs around 4,000 people. Most tax returns are processed between January and June each year, and for the IRS, this is the busiest time of year.

The facility manager at the Kansas City office is Joseph R. Campfield. He and his staff carry out all the maintenance tasks between July and December – the off-peak season. According to Campfield, the facility management staff then "spend the following six months trying not to interfere with the IRS activities. We try to be 'invisible' during that time."

The IRS office is notable for its green design. Its large windows and atriums allow in lots of daylight. It is divided into sections so that large parts of the building can be shut down during off-peak times.

Campfield began working at the site about four months after construction began in 2004. He familiarized himself with the building and met with the construction team. Consequently, he was able to influence aspects of the design. Many of the changes he asked for did not cost much to introduce during construction, but would have been expensive to put right once the building was completed.

To maximize energy efficiency, Campfield uses a building automation system (BAS) to monitor and control the building's systems via 26,000 control points. The BAS is able to monitor carbon monoxide levels in the car park, and controls an underfloor air distribution (UFAD) system. The building has been designed so that energy consumption can be shut down in any of its three wings independently. UFAD is used to identify unoccupied zones in the building, allowing energy to be conserved.

Facility management and computers

In many modern buildings, the job of maintenance has been assisted by computers. As discussed on page 39, a building automation system (BAS) is a network of electronic devices designed to monitor and control all the mechanical systems of a building. If a mechanical failure occurs, BAS provides maintenance staff with an email or text notification.

Facility managers can also be assisted by a building information model (BIM, see page 7). The BIM provides information on every structural or mechanical component of a building. If there is a leak on the third floor, the facility manager can look at the BIM and see if a water valve is located near by.

Health and safety

Health and safety policies vary from building to building. Procedures necessary in a chemical factory, for example, would not be appropriate in an office block. Nevertheless, there are basic health and safety principles that apply to all buildings – for example, the need to protect occupants from fire, flood, chemical or biological hazards, excessive noise or vibration, the maintenance of good air quality, and removal of potential causes of accident.

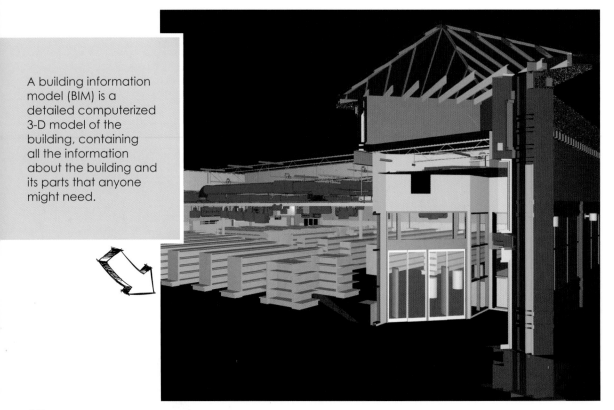

A building information model (BIM) is a detailed computerized 3-D model of the building, containing all the information about the building and its parts that anyone might need.

LEED AND SOLAIRE

Leadership in Energy and Environmental Design (LEED) is a system of ratings awarded for sustainable design, construction, and operation of buildings.

The Solaire, a 27-storey residential tower in New York, USA, has a LEED Gold certificate. It offers its residents hybrid rental cars, cycle parking, and electric vehicle charging. Gardens of native shrubs grow on its roof, helping to lower heating and cooling costs. It uses recycled wastewater for its cooling tower, low-flow toilets, and for irrigating its gardens. Automatic dimming lights, solar panels, and high-performance windows help cut its energy demand.

THE SOLAIRE USES:

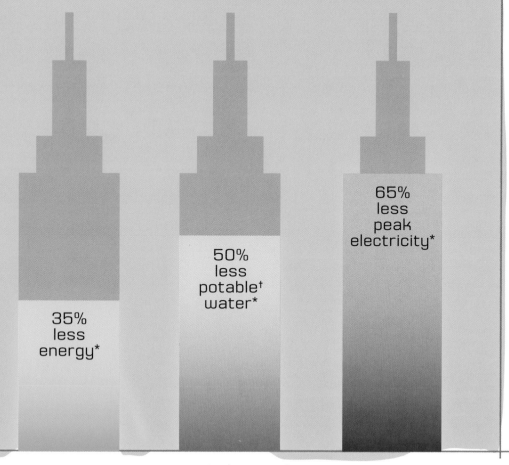

35%
less
energy*

50%
less
potable†
water*

65%
less
peak
electricity*

*less than an average building of this size and type
†potable water is water that is clean enough to drink

Fire prevention

Of all the health and safety issues, perhaps the greatest emphasis is placed on fire prevention. Fire prevention systems are built into most modern buildings at the design and construction stage, with the installation of passive fire protection (fire proofing, fire doors, and fire stops) and active fire protection (fire and smoke alarms, sprinkler systems, and extinguishers).

The facility manager is responsible for the maintenance and regular testing of active fire protection systems and also carrying out regular fire drills to ensure the building's occupants know what to do in the event of a fire. These efforts are expensive. In the United Kingdom, £3.3 billion was spent on fire protection for buildings in 2008. In that year, 475 people died in fires.

In the event of a building fire, the firefighters' chief responsibility is to save the lives of occupants and to prevent the spread of the fire to surrounding buildings.

Security

Security is about preventing unauthorized persons from gaining entry to a building. The type of security required depends very much on what kind of building it is and what it is used for. A bank, prison, or nuclear facility will require greater levels of security than, say, a village hall.

Those who design and maintain security systems must balance security needs against available resources and the needs of the building's users. In the case of high-security buildings, there are usually four layers of security:

- *Deterrence and delay*: warning signs, bright lights, and cameras outside to deter intruders, and high walls, vehicle barriers, and fences to delay their entry.
- *Access control*: locks on gates and doors. Many buildings now have electronic access control instead of traditional key-opening locks. A user's access rights can be limited to certain hours of the day and will expire after a certain number of months.
- *Detection and identification*: security alarms. These work by detecting changes in temperature caused by the presence of an object, or by detecting changes in frequency caused by motion. As well as setting off an alarm, the detectors can activate a camera.
- *Human response*: guards may be used at all the above stages. Guards may also be needed to physically confront and evict an intruder.

Security cameras can maintain 24-hour surveillance around a building.

WHAT HAVE WE LEARNED?

- Facility managers maintain buildings as functioning facilities and safe and healthy environments.
- Facility management may be assisted by computer systems such as BAS and BIM.
- Fire prevention systems must be regularly checked, tested, and maintained.

DEMOLITION AND DECONSTRUCTION

The final stage in any building's life cycle is its demolition. In this chapter, we will look at the steps that must be taken to demolish a building and the different methods of demolition. We will also look at the greener alternative to demolition – deconstruction.

First steps

Before a building can be demolished, consent must be sought and obtained from the local authority, the public must be notified, utilities disconnected, and the site fenced off. The next stage is to remove any hazardous materials, such as asbestos. Once that has been done, the demolition crew can move in.

This high-reach excavator is fitted with rotating hydraulic shears. These pulverise the concrete so the steel inside can be salvaged for reuse.

Non-explosive demolition

There are various methods of non-explosive demolition, some of which may be used in combination. The method or methods chosen will depend on the type of building.

- *Undermining*: low-rise buildings are often demolished by **undermining**. Hydraulic excavators dig into the base of the building's walls, causing it to collapse. The aim is to control the direction in which the building falls, so safety is maximized and cleaning up minimized.
- *Wrecking ball*: a crane equipped with a wrecking ball can reduce a building to a manageable height, after which undermining can take place. Wrecking balls weigh up to 6,000 kilograms (13,000 pounds). Their use is declining as the industry moves towards more controlled forms of demolition.
- *High-reach demolition*: high-reach excavators can be used to topple tall buildings. They have a demolition arm to which may be attached shears (to dismantle steel components), hammers (to shatter concrete), or crushers (to crush concrete and remove reinforcing steel).

These volunteers are dismantling houses wrecked by attacks on London during World War II.

CONTRAST THE PAST

Traditionally, most buildings were demolished over months using small hand tools. With the construction of larger, stronger buildings in the early 20th century, new demolition techniques had to be developed. This era saw the rise of the wrecking ball, supplemented by the use of explosives.

In the early 2000s, environmental considerations gave rise to a new trend: deconstruction. That is, dismantling in order to reuse or recycle components. Some see this as a return to earlier traditions. According to the environmental group, The Reuse People of America, "Humans have been salvaging their domiciles [homes] since the dawn of built shelters. Only in the last 50–60 years has machinery … made mechanical demolition of buildings the common practice."

More methods of demolition

Ramming: some buildings are demolished by being rammed by loaders, hydraulic excavators, or bulldozers, usually equipped with "rakes" – thick tubes of steel. If this method is carried out in built-up areas, neighbouring buildings must be protected from falling debris.

Vérinage: this French technique involves weakening the supports of the central floors of the building, causing the top part to collapse. The weight and momentum of this will also cause the bottom part to collapse.

Cut-and-take-down method: this method uses computer-controlled hydraulic jacks to support the bottom storey as the support beams are removed. The ceiling is then lowered on the jacks. The process is repeated for each storey. This method is safe to use in built-up areas. It is also less noisy and dusty than most methods and radically reduces the amount of landfill waste.

Demolition excavators have caterpillar tracks on their tyres to allow them to move over uneven ground. Their jointed arms (called backhoes or booms) can clear rubble and dig into walls.

Building implosions

Today, a common method of demolishing tall buildings is by implosion. In this method, the building does not erupt outwards. Instead, through a series of small explosions that destroy its structural supports, the building is pulled in on itself. If expertly done, it can fall into its own footprint. The demolition team often makes use of architectural plans, if they are available, and may develop 3-D computer models so they can see how the building will fall.

Before any implosion takes place, all items of value are removed from the building, as well as materials such as glass that can form deadly projectiles. Non-load-bearing walls are removed to aid the collapse. Holes are drilled in selected columns on the lower floors of the building, and explosives such as nitro-glycerine are placed in the holes. For safety and cost-effectiveness, as little explosive is used as possible. Columns, and sometimes whole floors, are wrapped in special fabric to prevent material from flying outwards.

Explosives are timed to go off at intervals to cause buildings to fall in a certain way. Sometimes, when the building to be demolished is touching another building, it needs to be peeled away in the opposite direction. This can be done by careful placing and timing of explosives.

This building is cracking and crumbling in on itself during a controlled implosion.

BUILDING TALK

Stacey Loizeaux, who works for Controlled Demolition, explains how building implosions work:

"The explosives are really just the catalyst. Largely what we use is gravity. And we're dealing with Class A explosives that are embedded into concrete – and that concrete flies. So, let's say your explosive is 17,000 feet per second – you've got a piece of concrete moving at that speed when you remove it from the structure. So we try to use the minimal amount to keep down the fly of debris for a safe operation."

To read more of this interview, go to: www.pbs.org/wgbh/nova/kaboom/loizeaux.html

Deconstruction

Just like architects and builders, the demolition industry has been trying to adopt greener approaches in recent years. Deconstruction has been described as "construction in reverse" because it involves dismantling a building, piece by piece. The aim is to recycle or reuse as much of the building's component materials as possible, so the minimum amount ends up going to landfill.

Unlike demolition, which is all about clearing a site as quickly as possible, deconstruction is slow and labour-intensive. Reusable parts need to be removed carefully to avoid damaging them. However, deconstruction tends to be cheaper than demolition because it does not require the use of heavy machinery, and because costs can be recouped by reselling items.

ECO IMPACT
- Construction and demolition waste in England (2008): 86.9 million tonnes
- Demolition waste recycled in England (estimate, 2008): 53 million tonnes
- Number of demolition companies in the United Kingdom (2011): 300
- Number of people working in demolition in the United Kingdom (2011): 3,400

By extending the life of building materials, deconstruction reduces the need to mine or harvest new materials. It also reduces greenhouse gas emissions caused by the burning or decomposition of waste in landfills and waste incinerators. In 2008, 53 million tonnes of construction and demolition waste produced in England was recycled and 11 million tonnes was used for land reclamation, agricultural improvement, and infrastructure projects. Twenty-two million tonnes was sent to landfill.

Non-structural and structural deconstruction

Deconstruction is normally divided into non-structural and structural. Non-structural deconstruction involves stripping out elements such as doors, windows, fireplaces, baths, and appliances – objects that can be renovated, resold, and reused as they are. This is usually the first stage of any deconstruction project. Structural deconstruction means dismantling the structural components of a building, such as the walls, floors, and roof. The crew usually begins with the roof and works down towards the foundation.

The individual materials that make up the structural components – brick, wood, and concrete, for example – are separated out and then sent for recycling. Today, architects are "designing for deconstruction", choosing materials based on their ability to be reused and recycled when the building reaches the end of its life.

This student accommodation block at the University of Netherlands in Utrecht, has a modular construction designed for deconstruction. At the end of its useful life, it will be dismantled and its materials will be reused or recycled.

WHAT HAVE WE LEARNED?

- There are many different ways of demolishing a building.
- Implosions require the careful placing of a small number of explosives, and work by using gravity.
- Deconstruction takes longer than demolition but is cheaper and better for the environment.

TIMELINE

7500 BC	Earliest known bricks are used at Tell Aswad, near Damascus, Syria.
3500 BC	Glass is invented in Mesopotamia.
2500 BC	Evidence suggests that prehistoric surveyors planned Stonehenge using peg and rope geometry.
AD 1400s	Buildings start to be identified with specific architects, marking the beginning of architecture as a profession.
1571	The first description of the surveying tool, the theodolite, is found in *Pantometria* by Leonard Diggs.
1773	The Holy Trinity Cathedral in Waterford, Ireland, is blown up, the first documented example of building implosion.
1820s	Quantity surveying emerges as a profession.
1824	Englishman Joseph Aspdin invents Portland Cement.
1849	Frenchman Joseph Monier invents reinforced concrete.
1852	Elisha Otis of the United States invents the safety lift.
1856	Englishman Henry Bessemer converts pig iron into steel.
1875	Earthquake engineering begins in Japan.
1884	Steel has virtually replaced iron as a construction material.
1885	The Home Insurance Building, the first steel-framed skyscraper, is built in Chicago, USA.
1894	Augustine Sackett of the United States invents plasterboard.
1906	The first documented death from exposure to asbestos occurs.
1950s	Plasterboard comes into common use.
1959	Englishman Alistair Pilkington invents "float glass".
1963	Sketchpad, the first CAD system with a graphical user interface, is developed.
1974	The Health and Safety Commission is established in the United Kingdom, taking steps to secure the health and safety of workers, including those in the construction industry.
1975	CAD systems that can be used for 3-D modelling begin to be used.
1987	The era of sustainable architecture begins with the publication of *Our Common Future*, a United Nations report by the World Commission on Environment and Development.
1987	ArchiCAD, the first BIM product, is released.
1990s	CAD systems are widely adopted by architectural offices.
1998	Leadership in Energy and Environmental Design (LEED) is founded.
1998	The J. L. Hudson Building in Detroit, USA, becomes the largest building ever imploded.
2008	BIM applications are released that enable real-time views of plans, sections, and elevations.

Buildings constructed in ancient and medieval times often survived for hundreds of years, and saw refurbishment, rebuilding, and changes of use – they had a product life cycle, just as buildings do today. We can also recognise building techniques that people in the past used. This painting of a medieval building shows a roof frame that a modern-day roofer would find familiar. You can also see cranes and pulleys being used.

GLOSSARY

acidification build-up of acids in the soil, such as nitric or sulphuric acid, due to pollution

adobe type of clay used as a building material, commonly in the form of sun-dried bricks

aggregate pieces of broken or crushed stone or gravel used to make concrete

alloy metal made by combining two or more metallic elements, usually in order to give greater strength or resistance to corrosion

asbestos heat-resistant fibrous mineral that can be used in insulating materials. The health risks associated with breathing in toxic asbestos particles have led to bans on its use in many parts of the world.

carbon dioxide colourless, odourless gas produced by burning carbon and organic compounds and by respiration

Computer-Aided Design (CAD) use of computer technology for the process of designing objects

crawlspace area of limited height under a building, giving access to wiring and plumbing

deconstruction dismantling of building components for the purpose of reuse and recycling

developer person who buys land to construct or renovate buildings with the aim of reselling at a profit

drywall type of board made from plaster, wood pulp, or other material, used to form interior walls of houses

ecological concerned with the relation of living organisms to one another and to their physical surroundings

excavator large machine used for removing soil from the ground on a building site, or for demolishing buildings

facility manager person responsible for the day-to-day operation of a building and for the health and safety of its occupants

feasibility study investigation that aims to look objectively at the strengths and weaknesses of a proposed business venture, such as a new building development

general contractor person in charge of the day-to-day management of a building site

greenhouse gas gas, such as carbon dioxide, that contributes to the greenhouse effect. The greenhouse effect is the trapping of the Sun's warmth in Earth's atmosphere.

heavy metals toxic metallic elements, such as mercury and lead

hydraulic operated by a liquid moving in a confined space

infrastructure buildings, roads, power supplies, and other facilities that a developed society needs to function

landfill place where waste material is buried and covered over with soil, especially as a method of filling in or extending usable land

load-bearing (especially of a wall) supporting much of the weight of the overlying parts of a building or other structure

Local Planning Authority (LPA) governmental institution that is authorized by law to carry out town planning functions for a particular locality in a country

masonry parts of a building that are made of stone

motion detector security device that can detect motion within a field of view, and convert it into an electric signal in order to trigger, for example, a light, camera, or alarm

rafter one of a number of internal beams that form the framework of a roof

reclamation retrieving or recovering (material) for reuse

renewable (of energy) can be used over time without running out

salvage retrieve, rescue, or preserve (property or material) from potential loss

seismic relating to earthquakes

slurry semi-liquid mixture, typically made up of fine particles of a substance suspended in water

stucco fine plaster used for coating wall surfaces or moulding into architectural decorations

subcontractor person or business that carries out work for a company as part of a larger project

survey process of accurately studying, measuring, and mapping an area of land

surveyor person whose profession is the surveying of land

sustainable conserving an ecological balance by not using up natural resources and adopting methods that avoid damaging the environment

synthetic human-made substances, made by chemical synthesis

topography natural contours of a piece of land; its three-dimensional shape

truss framework, usually consisting of rafters, posts, and struts, supporting a roof

undermining dig or excavate the base of a structure such as a building in order to make it collapse

BUILDING MATERIAL ASSESSMENT SYSTEM (BMAS)

The environmental impacts of building materials

An Australian system called Building Material Assessment System (BMAS) looks at how different materials compare in terms of their environmental impact during the five stages of the material's life cycle (extraction, manufacture, construction, use, and demolition). Materials are assessed according to:

- renewability of raw material
- damage to the environment during mining/harvesting of raw material
- water usage in, and air pollution caused by, manufacture
- energy consumed in transportation/erecting/assembling
- on-site waste/packaging
- maintenance required and environmental impact during life of building
- environmental impact of demolition; recyclability of demolished material.

The BMAS system has been used to compare the relative environmental impact of different types of wall, floor, and roof assemblies (the higher the number, the greater the environmental impact).

	BMAS scale
walls	
timber frame, plasterboard	7.2
steel frame, plasterboard	7.4
autoclaved aerated concrete blocks* (rendered)	20.6
clay bricks (rendered)	49.1
floors	
timber, brick piers, footings	41.9
concrete raft slab	74.4
roof	
timber frame, corrugated steel	5.2
timber frame, terracotta tile**	20.6

*A type of lightweight, precast, insulating block.

** Although steel has a higher environmental impact than terracotta, a lot more terracotta than steel is needed to build a roof, hence the higher impact of terracotta here.

FIND OUT MORE

Books

Architecture (Culture in Action), Jane Bingham (Raintree, 2010)
Hospitals (Buildings at Work), Elizabeth Encarnacion (QED Publishing, 2008)
Skyscrapers (Building Amazing Structures), Chris Oxlade
    (Heinemann Library, 2006)
Stadiums (Building Amazing Structures), Chris Oxlade
    (Heinemann Library, 2006)

Websites

www.greatbuildings.com/gbc/buildings.html
This list includes over 1,000 great buildings from around the world, complete with photographs, architectural information, and, in some cases, architectural drawings.

uiabee.riai.ie/index-en.html
This International Union of Architects (UIA) website is devoted to helping teachers and architects show young people what makes good architecture and a sustainable environment.

www.tomorrowsengineers.org
Visit this website to find out how to plan for a career in engineering.

Topics for further research

*   Research the design and construction of Masdar, Abu Dhabi's sustainable city. See the website: **www.masdarcity.ae/en**

*   Research the use and dangers of asbestos. What measures have governments taken to restrict the use of this material and safeguard the health of construction workers? See the website: **www.who.int/ipcs/ assessment/public_health/asbestos/en**

*   Imagine you have been asked to design and build an international airport terminal. Think about the needs of the people who will be using it and those affected by it. Think about the environment, health and safety, and security. What factors would you need to consider in the design and construction?

INDEX